CRYSTAL HEALING FOR THE CHAKRAS

A Beginner's Guide to the Chakras & Chakra Balancing with Crystals

ETHAN LAZZERINI

ISBN: 153358690X
ISBN-13: 978-1533586902

ALSO BY ETHAN LAZZERINI

Psychic Protection Crystals

The Modern Guide To Psychic Self-Defence With Crystals
For Empaths & Highly Sensitive People

Crystal Grids Power

Harness The Power of Crystals & Sacred Geometry for
Manifesting Abundance, Healing & Protection

CONTENTS

INTRODUCTION

Having a good understanding of the Chakra System will give you a really solid foundation for all crystal healing work you do in the future. This will deeply enhance your knowledge of crystals and help you with selecting the right ones for your needs.

I will guide you through the ladder of lights known as the Chakra System. We will explore each chakra one by one. Understand how the chakras relate to your mind, body, spirit and emotions.

Learn how to tell if your chakras are clear, balanced, weak or blocked. Find out which crystals relate to each chakra and how to use or make your own Chakra Crystal Set. You will learn practical step-by-step ways to clear, balance, align and activate the energy of your chakras with crystals.

This book takes you beyond the traditional seven Major Chakras. Discover the secrets of the Soul Star and Earth Star Chakras. I will also reveal to you special 'Chakra Hacks' that show you how to cleanse, balance or align all your chakras with just one crystal.

Before you delve deeper don't forget to download my free Ebook 'Discover Your Guardian Stone' which reveals your personal go-to crystal for psychic protection based on your astrological energy. It's only available on my website at the web address on the following page.

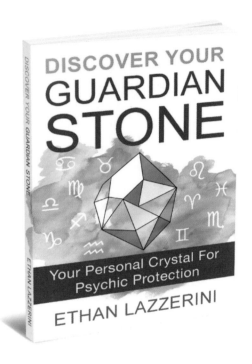

Get your Free Ebook when you sign up to my
Crystal Newsletter at:

www.ethanlazzerini.com/freegift

1

WHAT ARE CHAKRAS?

The Chakras are spiritual energy centers that lie along the spine. Knowledge of this was passed down to us over thousands of years through the ancient Hindu traditions of India. It has since spread around the World with the interest in energy healing, yoga and meditation.

What Does the Word Chakra Mean?

The word Chakra comes to us from the Sanskrit word commonly translated as "wheel". Ancient texts also depict them as sacred Lotus flowers. The Chakras are often seen clairvoyantly as being more like spinning vortices of light and energy. They have also been perceived as being different colours.

What do the Chakras do?

The chakras are a vital part of your energy body, they allow your life force to circulate within your physical body and aura (your energy field). Each chakra has its own area of focus and expression.

You could see them as levels of consciousness, which we express in different ways. Some chakras are more focused on physical concerns while others are more spiritual. If you are very focused on one area of your life it is likely that is your most active Chakra.

Your chakras give and receive energy constantly. If you have a lot of negative or disempowering thoughts it is likely that negative energy will build up in the associated chakra which can then manifest as recurring types of problems in our lives.

The same applies to chakras that become weak or underused. Some holistic healers believe that this could over time manifest as a health condition in the associated area of the physical body.

Chakras are also the system that psychic energy and insights travel through. By keeping the chakras clear you can strengthen your natural born intuition and develop your psychic abilities.

How Many Chakras are there?

There are hundreds of chakras within the body and aura. Some big, some small. The ones most people concern themselves with are the seven Major Chakras, which tend to have the biggest impact on who we are and how we live our lives.

I am going to include the addition of two extra chakras in this book as an introduction to the Higher Chakras. These two chakras are becoming more well known.

2

EXPLORING THE CHAKRA SYSTEM

Now let's look at the Chakra Chart on the next page to see where exactly the chakras are. It is helpful to understand the way the chakras work by splitting them into groups. Here is an overview to help you.

The Lower Chakras

These chakras are to be found in the lower half of the body. They include the Root Chakra, Sacral Chakra and the Solar Plexus Chakra. They vibrate at the lower end of the colour spectrum in the warmer colours.

The Lower Chakras represent our more down to earth aspects of the physical world including our connection to the Earth, physical security, sexuality and also how we interact with other people.

THE CHAKRA CHART

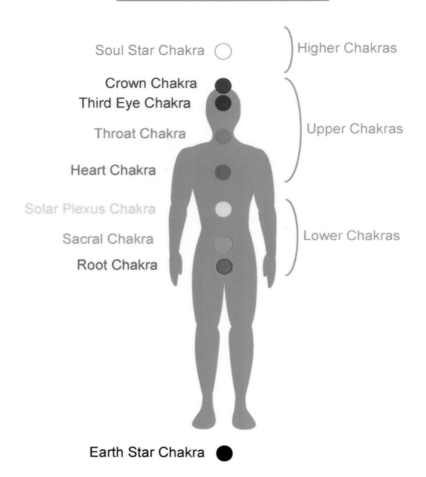

Soul Star Chakra) Higher Chakras

Crown Chakra
Third Eye Chakra
Throat Chakra } Upper Chakras
Heart Chakra

Solar Plexus Chakra
Sacral Chakra } Lower Chakras
Root Chakra

Earth Star Chakra

The Upper Chakras

These chakras are in the upper half of the body and head area. They include the Heart Chakra, Throat Chakra, Third Eye Chakra and the Crown Chakra. These chakras vibrate at a higher rate, manifesting as cooler or more airy colours.

The Upper Chakras are generally more spiritual in nature but also work with the emotions and the mind. They embody love, communication, intuition and connection to the divine.

The Higher Chakras

These chakras are located outside of the physical body and mostly above the Crown Chakra. They vibrate at a very high rate. Some consider these new chakras while others think they are actually ancient, with knowledge of them only just returning to us now.

The Higher Chakras are focused on the spiritual world and divine connections. Opinions on the exact workings of these chakras and colour associations do vary, as we are still learning about them.

For the purpose of this book I have been guided to include one that is located above the Crown Chakra called the Soul Star Chakra. There is also one below the feet called the Earth Star Chakra.

The Minor Chakras

There are even smaller chakras found all over the body that receive energy from the Major Chakras and distribute it. You have Minor Chakras on the palms of your hands, the soles of the feet and your knees for example.

The Palm Chakras receive their energy from the Heart Chakra. Energy from the Root Chakra travels down the legs to the Knee Chakras and out through the soles of the feet. The chakras on the feet are also connected to the Earth Star Chakra within the Earth.

Colour is Vibration

Notice how the colours of the seven Major Chakras are related to the order of colours in the visual light spectrum, like those you see within a rainbow. This all goes back to energy and how colours are created by light vibrating at different frequencies, low to high.

Despite these higher and lower vibrations it is important to remember that none of the chakras are 'bad' or any less important just like the colours of the rainbow. It is all about balance.

How Balanced and Clear Chakras Look

When working well a healthy, clear and balanced chakra will show this in its colour and brightness. Someone who can see chakras clairvoyantly would see them as bright and vibrant colours, with a gem like clarity.

How Unbalanced or Blocked Chakras Look

If a chakra becomes unbalanced from becoming blocked with negative energy or weak this is reflected in its vibration and colour. Someone who can see chakras clairvoyantly may see this as dark areas within the chakra, a dirty colour or a lack of clarity and brightness.

Exploring the Chakras

Now let's go deeper into the different qualities of each of the chakras. You will learn their traditional Sanskrit names, plus any alternative names they are known by. We will look at their associated colours and physical body associations.

I have separated the chakra qualities to show the different ways they may affect us when they are balanced or unbalanced. Please note an imbalance may manifest from a chakra being weak, blocked or it could be over active.

The Earth Star Chakra

Location: About six inches below the feet

Colours: Black, Dark Brown

Body Associations: Feet

Chakra Group: Higher Chakras

Rules: Anchors and aligns all chakras, Union with Gaia, Sacred Sites, Ley Lines, The Mineral Kingdom, Inner Earth

When Clear and Balanced:

Connected to the Earth, Gaia, Crystals and the Land, Seeing Earth as a conscious being, Drawn to Sacred Sites, Can sense Earth energies such as Ley Lines

When Unbalanced or Blocked:

No connection to the Earth, Gaia, Crystals or the Land, Do not view the Earth as conscious in any way, No interest in Sacred Sites, Do not believe in or sense Earth energies

The Root Chakra

Alternative Names: The First Chakra, The Base Chakra

Sanskrit Name: Muladhara

Location: The base of the spine

Colours: Red

Glands: Adrenals

Body Associations: Lower back, Colon, Legs, feet

Chakra Group: Major Chakras, Lower Chakras

Rules: Grounding, Security, Money, Survival

Spiritual: Kundalini, Connection to Gaia, Earth Based Spirituality, Feng Shui

When Clear and Balanced:

Connected to the Earth and nature, Feeling grounded, Healthy finances, Able to manifest what you need, Feeling safe and secure, Good physical health and fitness, Having lots of energy, Feeling comfortable in your own skin

When Unbalanced or Blocked:

Disconnected from the Earth and nature, Ungrounded, Feeling scattered, Overly fearful, Fear of nature or natural disasters, Frequent money troubles, Work and career fears, Trouble manifesting, Bad physical health, Low energy, Insecurity, Uncomfortable in your own skin, Materialistic

The Sacral Chakra

Alternative Names: The Second Chakra

Sanskrit Name: Svadhisthana

Location: Below the navel, a few inches above the Root Chakra

Colours: Orange

Glands: Ovaries or Gonads

Body Associations: Sexual Organs, Kidneys, Bladder, Womb

Chakra Group: Major Chakras, Lower Chakras

Rules: Creativity, Sexuality, Physical Desires

Spiritual: Sacred Sexuality, Male and Female Balance, Co Creation

When Clear and Balanced:

Good creative flow, Having creative outlets, Healthy sexual relationships, Knowing who you are, Feeling attractive

When Unbalanced or Blocked:

Blocked creative expression, Lack of creativity, Intimacy issues, Low sexual drive, Empty sexual relationships, Sexual addiction, Overly preoccupied with your image

The Solar Plexus Chakra

Alternative Names: The Third Chakra, The Navel Chakra

Sanskrit Name: Manipura

Location: Between the ribcage and navel or behind the navel

Colours: Yellow or Gold

Glands: Pancreas

Body Associations: Digestive System, Liver, Pancreas

Chakra Group: Major Chakras, Lower Chakras

Rules: Personal Power, Willpower, Control

Spiritual: Divine Soverignity, Spiritual Power

When Clear and Balanced:

Feeling empowered, Confident, Strong willpower, Self Belief, Self worth, Feeling in control of your life, Good leadership qualities, Life is what you make it beliefs, Enjoys empowering others

When Unbalanced or Blocked:

Feeling disempowered, Fear of personal power, Lack of self confidence, Low self esteem, Don't believe in themselves, Weak willpower, Life happens to me beliefs, Fear of authority, Being a control freak, Wanting power over others, Self centred

The Heart Chakra

Alternative Names: The Fourth Chakra, The Heart Centre

Sanskrit Name: Anahata

Location: The middle of the chest area

Colours: Green or Pink

Glands: Thymus

Body Associations: Heart, Chest, Lungs, Upper Back, Shoulders, Arms, Hands

Chakra Group: Major Chakras, Upper Chakras

Rules: Love, Relationships, Compassion, Emotions, Your Feelings

Spiritual: Clairsentience, Divine Love, Twin Flame Connection

When Clear and Balanced:

Able to have loving relationships, Balanced relationships, Loving yourself, Compassionate, Empathic, Unconditional love, Easier to forgive and forget, Seeing the good in people, Able to express emotions comfortably

When Unbalanced or Blocked:

Unloving relationships, Inharmonious relationships, Fear of love, Not loving yourself, Lack of compassion, Lack of empathy, Possessiveness, Obsession with someone, Co-dependency, Carrying a broken heart, Unable to forgive, Carrying grudges, Hateful beliefs, Emotionally closed, Holding onto grief

The Throat Chakra

Alternative Names: The Fifth Chakra

Sanskrit Name: Vishuddha

Location: Throat, Adams apple

Colours: Blue or Turquoise

Glands: Thyroid, Parathyroid

Body Associations: Neck, Throat, Mouth, Ears, Jaw

Chakra Group: Major Chakras, Upper Chakras

Rules: Verbal Communication, Written Communication

Spiritual: Channeling, Spiritual Teaching, Clairaudience, Mantras, Affirmations

When Clear and Balanced:

Clear communication, Speaking your truth, Honesty, Good teaching or speaking skills, Will ask for help, Good listener, Write or want to write

When Unbalanced or Blocked:

Communication problems, Unable to speak up, Shyness, Fear of asking for help, Bluntness, Dishonesty, Not listening, Writers block, Fears about teaching or writing

The Third Eye Chakra

Alternative Names: The Sixth Chakra, The Brow Chakra

Sanskrit Name: Ajna

Location: Between and above the Eyebrows

Colours: Indigo

Glands: Pineal, Pituitary

Body Associations: Eyes, Forehead

Chakra Group: Major Chakras, Upper Chakras

Rules: Vision, Intuition, Perception

Spiritual: Clairvoyance, Psychic ability, Prophetic visions, Lucid dreams

When Clear and Balanced:

Mental clarity, Visual communicators, Artistic or appreciate art, Able to visualise well, Have vivid dreams, Clairvoyant abilities, Good intuition, Can see below the surface of things

When Unbalanced or Blocked:

Mental fog, Stuck in the mind, Artistic blocks, Closed minded about art, Struggle to visualise, Don't remember dreams, Fear of clairvoyant abilities, Poor intuition, Unable to control clairvoyant abilities

The Crown Chakra

Alternative Names: The Seventh Chakra

Sanskrit Name: Sahasrara

Location: Top of the head

Colours: Violet or White

Glands: Pineal

Body Associations: Head, Brain

Chakra Group: Major Chakras, Upper Chakras

Rules: Spiritual Connection, Consciousness, Inspiration

Spiritual: Claircognizance, Divine connection, Oneness, Guides and Angels

When Clear and Balanced:

Spiritually aware and awake, Feel connected to Source and the Universe, Receive divine messages, guidance or knowledge, Regularly inspired, Believe their life has a higher purpose, Want to make a difference in the World

When Unbalanced or Blocked:

Not spiritual, Believe spiritual wisdom comes only through another, Believe religious dogma or fundamentalism, Fear of spirituality or spiritual experiences, Fear of Source or God, Don't believe in a higher purpose to their life, Fear of spiritual beings

The Soul Star Chakra

Alternative Names: The Eighth Chakra

Location: About six inches above the top of the head

Colours: Clear, Rainbow, White or Magenta

Chakra Group: Higher Chakras

Rules: Past Lives, Life Purpose, Akashic Records, Karma

When Clear and Balanced:

Aware of past lives, May have past life memories, Believe they have a higher purpose, Able to access their personal Akashic Records or Life Blueprint

When Unbalanced or Blocked:

Believe we only live once, Do not believe they have a higher purpose to their life, Blocked past life memories

3

WORKING WITH CHAKRA CRYSTAL SETS

There are many ways to cleanse and balance your chakras such as with yoga, energy healing and meditation. Crystals work with these energy centres by tuning them into the right colour vibration and frequency. They also clear or transmute any negative or blocked energies from the chakras.

A set of crystals used exclusively for clearing or balancing the chakras is called a Chakra Crystal Set. I will show how to create a good Chakra Crystal Set using easily available crystals.

I will also give you a selection of other recommended crystals to choose from if you want to create your own custom set. Lastly I include my Chakra Crystals Cheat Sheet, so you can select from any crystals you have available. Even if you don't know what they are called!

Crystals and Chakra Associations

All crystals work with one or more of our chakras. Some crystals even work on all the chakras, which I will get to later in this book. All crystals have their own properties and unique frequency so you may find one crystal works better for you personally than another.

A good way to select crystals for a particular chakra if you have several options is to see which one draws you to it. Some crystals will attract you and others won't. We intuitively know what's best for us most of the time.

Finding a Chakra Crystal Set

You can get ready made Chakra Crystal Sets which usually come in a small bag or box from a metaphysical shop or online. They usually consist of seven polished crystals for each of the seven Major Chakras in the form of Tumble Stones.

There are some specialist Chakra Crystal Sets that are made from crystal discs that have been etched with the seven Sanskrit symbols. When selecting sets look for ones that do not use large crystals or contain very round stones that could slip off your body.

Tip: Look for medium to small Tumble Stones that have a nice flat side making them more stable and secure.

A Good Chakra Crystal Set:

This Chakra Crystal Set is a good place to start if you want to select your own crystals. Most ready made sets will be very similar to these seven crystals. I have also included optional but recommended crystals for those wishing to work with their Soul Star and Earth Star Chakras. They will increase your spiritual connection and help align all the chakras.

If you already have a Chakra Crystal Set you can upgrade it by adding two more crystals for the Higher Chakras. If you can't find any of these crystals you can easily substitute them for any of the crystals in the following section by selecting a replacement for the specific chakra it is for. See the Chakra Crystal Set photo below for examples of these crystals.

Amethyst (Violet) for the Crown Chakra

Lapis Lazuli (Dark Blue & Gold) for the Third Eye Chakra

Blue Lace Agate (Light Blue) for the Throat Chakra

Green Aventurine (Green) for the Heart Chakra

Tiger's Eye (Gold & Black) for the Solar Plexus Chakra

Carnelian (Orange) for the Sacral Chakra

Red Jasper (Red) for the Root Chakra

Optional Crystals:

Selenite (White) for the Soul Star Chakra

Black Tourmaline (Black) for the Earth Star Chakra

Creating Your Own Custom Chakra Crystal Set

This can be a lot of fun and will feel even more personalised as you can choose the exact combination of crystals yourself. I will give you a choice of recommended crystals based on the chakra they relate to.

Select one crystal for each of the seven Major Chakras to create your own chakra crystal set. I will go into more detail on some of these crystals in the following chapters. As before I have included two Higher Chakras for those who want to include them.

Please note that some crystals appear more than once for different chakras. Make sure each of your crystals are different from the others when selecting your crystals. In the next chapter we will look at preparing your Chakra Crystal Set.

For now it's time to go on a crystal quest and see which of these crystals resonates with you.

Soul Star Chakra Crystals:

Selenite, Herkimer Diamond, Quartz Crystal with a Rainbow inside, Angel Aura, Tibetan Clear Quartz, Rubellite, Star Sapphire, Lemurian Seed, Sugilite

Crown Chakra Crystals:

Amethyst, Chevron Amethyst, Quartz, Danburite, Sugilite, Purple Jade, Charioite, Lepidolite

Third Eye Chakra Crystals:

Lapis Lazuli, Sodalite, Amethyst, Sapphire, Tanzanite, Covellite, Azurite, Iolite, Iolite Sunstone, Herkimer Diamond

Throat Chakra Crystals:

Blue Lace Agate, Turquoise, Aquamarine, Blue Aventurine, Blue Topaz, Larimar, Angelite, Blue Chalcedony, Blue Opal

Heart Chakra Crystals:

Green Aventurine, Amazonite, Green Jade, Emerald, Rose Quartz, Pink Opal, Green Tourmaline, Chrysoprase, Malachite, Peridot, Rhodochrosite

Solar Plexus Chakra Crystals:

Tigers Eye, Citrine, Yellow Jasper, Honey Calcite, Yellow Opal, Heliodor

Sacral Chakra Crystals:

Carnelian, Orange Calcite, Tangerine Quartz, Peach Aventurine

Root Chakra Crystals:

Red Jasper, Hematite, Garnet, Ruby, Red Tourmaline, Mahogany Obsidian, Shiva Lingam, Bronzite

Earth Star Chakra Crystals:

Black Tourmaline, Smoky Quartz, Tibetan Black Quartz, Black Jade, Hematite, Magnetite, Black Obsidian, Chrysanthemum Stone

Chakra Crystals Cheat Sheet

Finding specific crystals can take some time. As I said earlier all crystals relate to the chakras. You may even have crystals, which you do not know the name of which you would still like to use.

The following easy to use guide will show you how to select crystals for each chakra based on their colour vibration. This is a general guide but it may be helpful.

Soul Star Chakra - White, Rainbow and Magenta Crystals

Crown Chakra - Purple, Clear and White Crystals

Third Eye Chakra - Indigo and Dark Blue Crystals

Throat Chakra - Light Blue and Blue Green Crystals

Heart Chakra - Green and Pink Crystals

Solar Plexus Chakra - Yellow and Golden Crystals

Sacral Chakra - Orange Crystals

Root Chakra - Red, Brown, Silver and Black Crystals

Earth Star Chakra - Black and Silver Crystals

4

PREPARING YOUR
CHAKRA CRYSTAL SET

In this chapter I will show you an easy way to cleanse your crystals and then consecrate and program them before you first use them. Ideally you want to use your Chakra Crystal Set only for chakra balancing. You can create a dedicated Chakra Crystal Set programmed with your intentions to cleanse and balance all chakras.

Cleansing Crystals

Whether you are using brand new crystals, a Chakra Crystal Set you just bought or crystals you already own it is important to cleanse them before use. By cleansing I mean clear any energies they may have picked up while in a shop, from any previous owners, through their travels or from past uses.

There are quite a lot of ways to clear your crystals of any negative or unwanted energy. If you are already familiar with crystal healing you may already have your own ways. Please do use the method you prefer.

For those of you who are new to this I will show you an easy method that you can do without any additional items or waiting for a full Moon. We are going to be using the energy of Universal White Light. Anyone can do this, there are no special qualifications or certificates required!

How To Cleanse Your Crystals With Universal White Light

1.   Find a quiet place where you will not be disturbed. Sit down with your legs crossed if you can.

2.   Hold your crystals in your hands. One hand over the other if possible or cupped.

3.   Close your eyes and visualise a beam of pure white light coming down from above into your Crown Chakra down to the Heart Chakra. Moving out along your arms and into your hands.

4.   See this Universal white light in your minds eye filling the crystals and surrounding the crystals.

5.   Focus on clearing them as you say out loud or in your head "I cleanse, purify and rebalance these crystals of all negative, unbalanced or fear based energies now"

6.   When you feel this has been done, open your eyes. You may need to take some time before you get up again.

Consecrating and Programming Crystals

It is a good idea to consecrate new crystals. This is also called dedicating and is a form of programming. Consecrating is really just setting your intention so that the crystal works for your highest good.

Programming is a way to direct and use the energy of a crystal for a very specific purpose. Your Chakra Crystal Set was put together for a specific reason. I am going to show you how to dedicate and program your crystals for the purpose of cleansing and balancing the chakras.

You only need to do this once before you first use your Chakra Crystal Set. If you already have a Chakra Crystal Set the following procedure should really improve their effectiveness.

How To Consecrate and Program Your Chakra Crystal Set

1.   Find a quiet place where you will not be disturbed. Sit down with your legs crossed if you can.

2.   Hold your Chakra Crystal Set in both hands in front of you just above eye level.

3.   Say out loud or to yourself "I dedicate these crystals to the original creator Source (Or God, Goddess, Universe etc.) May these crystals serve and only serve my highest and greatest good and the highest and greatest good of all"

4.   Next clearly focus on the crystals while saying out loud or to yourself "I program these crystals to cleanse and rebalance all my chakras"

Storing Your Chakra Crystal Set

If you created your own Chakra Crystal Set I do recommend you have a special bag or box to store and protect your crystals when not in use. You can use a soft pouch to store them in or a small box. Choose what feels right for you.

5

HOW TO CLEANSE & BALANCE YOUR CHAKRAS WITH CRYSTALS

Now your Chakra Crystal Set has been cleansed, consecrated and programmed it is all ready for use. I am going to show you step by step how to use a Chakra Crystal Set to clear and balance your chakras. I have incorporated a visualisation to help ground you so the energies can flow more freely.

How to Use Your Chakra Crystal Set

Before you begin start by making sure you will not be disturbed. You need to be in a quiet and private place where you can comfortably lie down. You could use your bed. Have your Chakra Crystal Set within reach.

You may find it easier to have all the crystals in a row next to you in the order they will be placed on and around your body.

1.   Lay down facing up and get into a comfortable position.

2.   Sit up and place your first chakra crystal in position. Either around six inches below your feet for the Earth Star Chakra or over your Root Chakra. You can also place your Root Chakra crystal under you if that is easier.

3.   Now lay back and work your way up from here placing each crystal on your body in the locations of the chakras.

4.   Once done close your eyes and take some deep breaths.

5.   Visualise yourself as being a large strong tree with roots going deep into the Earth.

6.   See your roots reaching the very centre of the Earth where they wrap around a large Iron crystal.

7.   Now just relax and allow the crystals to do their work. Your chakras should be cleansed and rebalanced in about 10 minutes.

8.   Afterwards open your eyes and take a few moments before removing the crystals from your body and getting up again.

With practice all this will become like second nature to you. I recommend doing chakra balancing once a week if possible to get the most out of it. With regular clearing and balancing you may notice your psychic abilities start to get stronger or awaken.

You can do this as often as you want or feel you need to. It's a good idea to cleanse our chakras when you feel stressed or are going through big changes in your life. This helps you feel more balanced and less attached to past situations that no longer serve you.

Remember to Cleanse Your Chakra Crystal Set

Whenever you use crystals for healing or place them within your chakras they will absorb energies. These energies could be unbalanced, negative or hold a strong emotional charge. At the very least they will reduce the effectiveness of the crystal by clogging it up.

Always cleanse your Chakra Crystal Set after each use. You can use any method you prefer or cleanse with Universal White Light as described earlier. After cleansing your crystals you can put them safely back into their bag or box until their next use.

6

ACTIVATING YOUR CHAKRAS WITH CRYSTALS

I will now show you how to select crystals based on their chakra association. This is a very useful way to choose crystals for every day life or for current issues you are working on. You can use crystals when you need to tap into your inner power or bring about change.

Let's say you have ongoing challenges you can now see are related to a certain chakra. Regular chakra clearing and balancing will help but you may need extra help and support between chakra balancing sessions.

As explained earlier all crystals have chakra associations. All chakras govern different areas of our lives, emotions or abilities. Once you get more familiar with the chakras you will start to see how they can relate to all kinds of things.

Choosing Crystals by Chakra Association

Understanding your chakras can really help you make sense of how you feel and experience life. By knowing which chakra to work on, you can easily select the right crystals to work with.

You may not even have a blocked chakra but feel you could do with a boost in a certain area of your life. Let's say you are a bit shy and feel you need help speaking up more in social situations.

By checking the descriptions of the chakras earlier in this book you will see that this is a Throat Chakra related area. You could use a Throat Chakra crystal such as Blue Lace Agate to help activate this chakra and help you in expressing yourself more.

Maybe you lack the motivation to get out of the job that isn't paying you enough and you feel stuck in. This is a Root Chakra issue. Use a Root Chakra crystal such as Garnet to help motivate you to start taking action.

Think about just one area of your life where you would like some help with. All you need to do is find which chakra rules that life area. Look through the detailed chakra descriptions in the Chakra System chapter. You may want to look at the blocks to identify areas you need to work on. Then choose from any of the crystals I recommend for that chakra.

To make this even easier I will give you a quick overview of the general associations for each of the chakras below. We will also look at crystals that activate the upper, lower and higher chakra groups.

Chakra Associations Quick List

Here is a quick list of the general keyword associations for each of the chakras to help you get started or to familiarise yourself more. For more detail do read the full chakra descriptions.

Soul Star Chakra – Past Lives, Life Purpose, Akashic Records, Karma

Crown Chakra – Spiritual Connection, Consciousness, Inspiration

Third Eye Chakra - Vision, Intuition, Clairvoyance, Perception

Throat Chakra - Verbal Communication, Written Communication

Heart Chakra - Love, Relationships, Compassion, Emotions

Solar Plexus Chakra – Personal Power, Willpower, Self Confidence, Control

Sacral Chakra – Creativity, Sexuality, Physical Desires

Root Chakra – Grounding, Security, Survival, Money

Earth Star Chakra – The Earth, Gaia, Sacred Sites, Ley Lines

Crystals that Activate the Lower Chakras

The following crystals can be used to activate the Lower Chakra group. This is helpful when there are several issues relating to grounding, finances, energy and motivation. Or when all these qualities are needed.

Carnelian

Smoky Quartz

Goldstone

Flame Aura

Crystals that Activate the Upper Chakras

The following crystals can be used to activate the Upper Chakra group. This is helpful when there are several issues relating to communication, intuition and spirituality. Or when all these qualities are needed.

Amethyst

Blue John

Azeztulite

Gibeon Meteorite

Crystals that Activate the Higher Chakras

The following crystals can be used to activate the Higher Chakra group. This is helpful when there is a need for higher spiritual awareness, working with guides and angels or understanding your life purpose.

Lemurian Seed

Danburite

Angel Aura

Faden Quartz

Different Ways to Use Crystals

Once you have found which crystal relates to your need you are ready to start using it. You can carry the crystal with you by placing it in a small bag or pouch. Place this in your pocket. By having it on your person you have it within your aura or energy field.

The other way to use your crystal is by wearing jewellery made of that stone. This can be anything from a pendant, bracelet or a ring. Crystal jewellery also works by acting as a visual reminder and trigger to your subconscious mind.

Jewellery and the Chakras

The connection between gemstones, different parts of the body and the chakras is ancient. It is not essential that your jewellery be placed over the related chakra but it is something you may wish to explore.

The chakras, which are more easily accessible through necklaces, include the Throat Chakra with short necklaces and chokers. The Heart Chakra with mid length necklaces. The Solar Plexus Chakra with low hanging necklaces.

Earrings can activate the Throat Chakra. Anything placed over the forehead will work with the Third Eye. Luckily you don't need to wear a gold crown studded with Diamonds to open your Crown Chakra. Hats and headwear can be used to conceal a crystal if you are clever. Remember crystals do not need to be seen to work, this is a spiritual technology.

The hands can link to the Heart Chakra with bracelets or rings too. Broaches and pins can also work on the heart. An anklet can link to the Root Chakra and Earth Star Chakras.

The other way bracelets and rings can be used is following the theory that our non-dominant hand is receptive. To gain qualities you would wear a bracelet on that hand.

To release things you no longer need in your life you could use your dominant hand. This hand is also used for manifestation, helping or healing others as you are sending energies out.

7

CHAKRA HACKS: CRYSTALS THAT CLEANSE ALL THE CHAKRAS

The Mineral Kingdom is a library of healing light that we can all tap into. Just as some crystals work with a single chakra, many work with several chakras and a few work with all of them.

The crystals in the following chapters are part of my Chakra Hacks because they are multitaskers and energetic shortcuts. They can be used instead of a traditional Chakra Crystal Set or along side it.

Wearing or carrying these powerful crystals can help keep your chakras clear, balanced or aligned. They range from easily available crystals that should be in everyone's crystal collection such as Quartz to more rare and unusual stones for you to discover.

First we will look at the crystals that cleanse all your chakras. Then we will explore the different methods and techniques you can use to harness the energies of these crystals for clearing negative or blocked energies from your chakras.

Quartz Crystal

Usable Forms:

Tumble Stone, Crystal Point, Crystal Wand

Description:

Quartz is the most abundant crystal on the planet. It is clear to white in colour but the clear varieties have the most cleansing properties.

Cleansing Properties:

Clear Quartz purifies the chakras with white light. It anchors and transmits high vibration energies in a very direct and specific way. This crystal also absorbs negative energies locking them away from causing harm.

Angel Aura

Usable Forms:

Tumble Stone, Crystal Point

Description:

Also known as Opal Aura. This is Quartz crystal, which has been bonded with precious metals such as Silver and Titanium. This creates a clear coated crystal with iridescent pastel rainbow colours.

Cleansing Properties:

This cleansing crystal clears all the chakras with its high vibration angelic energy. It banishes lower energies and also balances the chakras with its rainbow light.

Libyan Desert Glass

Usable Forms:

Unpolished Crystal

Description:

Also known as Libyan Gold Tektite. These stones were created by an ancient meteor impact in the Sahara Desert sands. This is a cloudy golden crystal with a matte surface. It has a rippled or crater like exterior.

Cleansing Properties:

Creates an influx of detoxifying golden light, which cleanses all the chakras. Very effective on badly clogged up chakras or stubborn energy blocks.

Tibetan Black Quartz

Usable Forms:

Crystal Point

Description:

Also known as Tibetan Quartz and Tibetan Black Spot Quartz. These crystals mostly grow as double terminated Crystal Points in the Mountains of the Himalayas. They are smoky coloured and many have black carbon inclusions or phantom formations inside them.

Cleansing Properties:

Tibetan Black Quartz absorbs negative energies from the chakras and aura like a sponge. These crystals transmute these energies but still need to be cleared as they can become overloaded sometimes.

Selenite

Usable Forms:

Tumble Stone, Unpolished Crystal, Crystal Wand

Description:

A delicate white crystal that was named after the Greek Goddess of the Moon, Selene. It has a crystalline structure that catches the light and makes it shimmer like moonlight.

Cleansing Properties:

Perhaps not surprisingly this crystal accesses the purifying powers of the Moon. Selenite sends a shower of cleansing celestial light through the chakras. It washes away negative or blocked energies with ease.

Serpentine

Usable Forms:

Tumble Stone, Crystal Wand

Description:

There are many varieties of Serpentine but it is commonly green to yellow green in colour. It can be an opaque or translucent stone. Some varieties have a snakeskin like pattern, which is where it got its name.

Cleansing Properties:

Serpentine specializes in clearing all the chakras and the luminous pathway that connects them. Its spiralling green light detoxifies dense and harmful energies and makes way for new light to enter.

Moldavite

Usable Forms:

Unpolished Crystal

Description:

These rare forms of Tektite were created by a massive meteor impact millions of years ago in what is now the Czech Republic. These glassy stones are an earthy dark green colour with a ruffled surface.

Cleansing Properties:

This crystal is not for the faint hearted. Moldavite is one of the most powerful cleansing crystals on the Planet. It rapidly flushes the entire Chakra System with its emerald green fire. This is another powerful cleanser and detoxifier of stuck or negative energies.

Ways to Use a Single Crystal to Cleanse Your Chakras

The most effective method to use these deeply cleansing crystals is to place them directly into the chakras or use them in meditation. Most these crystals are available as Tumble Stones or polished crystals, but there are some other options you may want to explore.

First we will look at a method you will be more familiar with which uses a Tumble Stone or polished crystal. If you do not wish to include the Soul Star or Earth Star Chakras in any of these methods you can just skip to the next chakra.

How to Cleanse Your Chakras with a Single Tumble Stone (Laying Down)

As with selecting crystals for a Chakra Crystal Set, make sure your crystal has at least one flat side so that it can be laid on the body securely. If the crystal you have does not come as a Tumble Stone use a polished or unpolished crystal.

1.   Find a quiet and comfortable place to lie down.

2.   Place your crystal about 6" below your feet within the location of the Earth Star Chakra.

3.   Lay down facing up and get into a comfortable position. Take a few deep breaths.

4.   Close your eyes and visualise yourself as being a large

strong tree with roots going deep into the Earth.

5.   See your roots reaching the very centre of the Earth where they wrap around a large Iron crystal.

6.   Sit up and move the crystal to your Root Chaka location. Lay back and relax for a about a minute or longer if you prefer.

7.   Then move the crystal up to the Sacral Chakra. Continue up the chakras leaving the crystal on each chakra for about a minute.

8.   Lastly place the crystal about 6" above the top of your head for the Soul Star Chakra.

9.   Open your eyes and take a few moments before getting up again.

How to Cleanse Your Chakras with a Single Tumble Stone (Sitting)

Similar to the method above but you will have to use your arms in this one. With practice this will become easier like a Yoga pose.

1.   Sit down with your legs crossed or on a chair and take a few deep breaths.

2.   Place your crystal on the floor, either between your legs or

under the chair. This is for the Earth Star Chakra.

3.   Visualise yourself as being a large strong tree with roots going deep into the Earth.

4.   See your roots reaching the very centre of the Earth where they wrap around a large Iron crystal.

5.   Next with both hands, hold your crystal in the position of your Root Chakra. Close your eyes and hold it there for about a minute or longer if you wish.

6.   Continue raising the crystal up through all the chakras. Spending about a minute with each one.

7.   For the Soul Star Chakra you will have to hold it with both hands about 6" above the head. Your arms should form a circular shape.

8.   Once finished put the crystal down safely. Raise your arms and shake them out.

9.   Open your eyes and take a few moments before getting up again.

Working with Crystal Points and Wands

Some crystals can be found in their natural crystal formation such as a Crystal Point. These are usually six sided with a point at one or both ends. Crystal Wands are usually crystals that have been cut and polished with facets similar to a natural Crystal Point. Some wands are smooth with no facets. These are called Crystal Massage Wands.

Tumble Stones emit energies in all directions but Crystal Points or cut Crystal Wands direct and focus energy through the tip. This makes them very popular with Crystal Healers as their energies can be directed towards the chakras without placement for example.

How to Cleanse Your Chakras with a Crystal Point or Wand

Working on yourself with a Crystal Point or Crystal Wand is more involved than using a Chakra Crystal Set. You may of course get a like-minded friend to use the crystal on your chakras.

1.   Sit down with your legs crossed or on a chair while holding your crystal in your dominant hand.

2.   Close your eyes and take a few deep breaths.

3.   Visualise yourself as being a large strong tree with roots going deep into the Earth.

4.   See your roots reaching the very centre of the Earth where they wrap around a large Iron crystal.

5.   Open your eyes, lower your hand and point your crystal

down towards the floor to the location of the Earth Star Chakra somewhere below your feet.

6.   In a small clockwise circular motion direct your crystal towards this chakra for about one minute or longer if you wish.

7.   Next move to the Root Chakra. You can point the crystal inwards now towards this area and again use circular motions for about a minute.

8.   Continue up through all the Major Chakras, clearing them one by one. For the Crown Chakra you can point the crystal downward towards the top of your head.

9.   For the Soul Star Chakra point the crystal upwards, just above the top of your head directing it in a circular motion as before. Take a few moments before getting up again.

How to Cleanse Your Chakras with a Single Crystal in Meditation

Meditations and visualisations are increasingly popular methods to cleanse and balance the chakras. You can use any form of chakra clearing crystal. With a natural Crystal Point or Crystal Wand, have the crystal pointing upwards in your hands.

1.   Sit down with your legs crossed or on a chair and close your eyes.

2.   Hold your crystal in your hands on your lap and take a few deep breaths.

3.   Visualise yourself as being a large strong tree with roots going deep into the Earth.

4.   See your roots reaching the very centre of the Earth where they wrap around a large Iron crystal.

5.   Focus on the crystal you are holding and visualise it begin to glow with light.

6.   Visualise a bright white laser beam descending into your Soul Star Chakra. For about a minute see this chakra shining like a white star.

7.   Now see this beam of light moving down into your Crown Chakra and this also shines like a bright star. Repeat this process down through all the chakras. Spending about a minute with each one.

8.   Open your eyes and take a few moments before getting up again.

8

CHAKRA HACKS: CRYSTALS THAT BALANCE ALL THE CHAKRAS

Cleansing our chakras will help bring them back into balance but sometimes there is no blockage or negative energy in the chakra. It may be that a chakra is just very weak, sluggish or in some cases it could even be over active.

The following carefully chosen crystals and crystal healing methods will help bring all your chakras back into balance.

Turquoise

Usable Forms:

Tumble Stone, Unpolished Crystal

Description:

This stone ranges from sky blue to blue green. It can have darker veins or some mottling with brown or white. Genuine Turquoise is much sought after and has been mined for thousands of years.

Balancing Properties:

This is a gentle healing crystal that balances your energy on many levels. Turquoise slows down over active chakras and brings sluggish chakras back into a healthy balance again.

Fluorite

Usable Forms:

Tumble Stone, Unpolished Crystal, Crystal Wand

Description:

This magical crystal comes in a variety of clear colours. It is often banded or a mixture of colours. Fluorite can be clear, purple, blue, green, yellow and white. For Chakra Balancing purposes look for a mixture of at least two colours or more. The mixed Fluorite is sometimes called Rainbow Fluorite.

Balancing Properties:

When Fluorite is placed within the chakras it quickly works to bring the energies back into balance and harmony with each other. Fluorite also balances all the layers of the aura.

Ammolite

Usable Forms:

Polished Crystal, Unpolished Crystal

Description:

Also known as Opalized Ammonite. This is an Ammonite fossil that has gleaming bright colours caused by mineralization over thousands of years. Ammolite was once an ancient sea creature, but is now a gemstone.

Balancing Properties:

Ammolite plugs you into the Universal life force that harmonises and balances your aura. It spiritually attunes each Chakra to its optimum frequency and colour vibration.

Quartz Crystal with a Rainbow

Usable Forms:

Tumble Stone, Crystal Point, Crystal Wand

Description:

This feature is caused by a natural internal flaw within a clear Quartz crystal that produces a rainbow colour effect. It is only noticeable when the flaw catches the light at the right angle so always check your crystals for rainbows!

Balancing Properties:

This type of clear Quartz specialises in balancing the chakras and all the layers of the aura. These crystals work on many levels and very quickly bring your energies back into a healthy balance again.

Gaia Stone

Usable Forms:

Polished Stone

Description:

Gaia Stone is created with the ash from a volcanic eruption at Mount St Helens in the USA. This man made gemstone is similar in composition to Obsidian, a volcanic glass. Gaia Stone is clear and has a deep emerald green colour.

Balancing Properties:

Gaia Stone harmonises you with the natural order and energies of the Earth. Its healing emerald green rays bring balance to the energy centres, balancing all the Chakras in a gentle way.

Angel Aura

Usable Forms:

Tumble Stone, Crystal Point

Description:

Also known as Opal Aura. This is Quartz crystal, which has been bonded with precious metals such as Silver and Titanium. This creates a clear coated crystal with iridescent pastel rainbow colours.

Cleansing Properties:

This ethereal crystal tunes and balances all the chakras with its rainbow energy. It banishes lower energies and also clears the chakras with its high vibration angelic light.

Spectrolite

Usable Forms:

Tumble Stone, Polished Stone

Description:

Genuine Spectrolite is a unique variety of Labradorite only found in Finland. It is black with intense and metallic colours, which shift and shine when it catches the light. Unlike common grey Labradorite it can be found in all colours of the spectrum.

Balancing Properties:

Mystical Spectrolite sends beams of multicoloured light deep into the chakras. It tunes the chakra to a balanced but higher vibration. This stone works to align the chakras with the Earth and the greater Universe.

Ways to Use a Single Crystal to Balance all the Chakras

Wearing or carrying any of these harmonious crystals will help keep your chakras balanced. The most effective method to use these crystals is to put them directly in the chakras or use them in meditation.

The following methods are similar to the previous chapter. As always if you do not wish to include the Soul Star or Earth Star Chakras in any of these methods you can just skip to the next chakra.

How to Balance Your Chakras with a Single Tumble Stone (Laying Down)

As with selecting crystals for a Chakra Crystal Set make sure your crystal has at least one flat side so that it can be laid on the body securely. If the crystal you have does not come as a Tumble Stone use a polished or unpolished stone.

1.   Find a quiet comfortable place to lie down.

2.   Place your crystal about 6" below your feet within the location of the Earth Star Chakra.

3.   Lay down facing up and get into a comfortable position. Take a few deep breaths.

4.   Close your eyes and visualise yourself as being a large strong tree with roots going deep into the Earth.

5.   See your roots reaching the very centre of the Earth where they wrap around a large Iron crystal.

6.   Sit up and move the crystal to your Root Chaka location. Lay back and relax for a about a minute or longer if you prefer.

7.   Then move the crystal up to the Sacral Chakra. Continue up the chakras leaving the crystal on each chakra for about a minute.

8.   Lastly place the crystal about 6" above the top of your head for the Soul Star Chakra.

9.   Open your eyes and take a few moments before getting up again.

How to Balance Your Chakras with a Single Tumble Stone (Sitting)

Similar to the method above but you will have to use your arms in this one. With practice this will become easier like a Yoga pose.

1.   Sit down with your legs crossed or on a chair and take a few deep breaths.

CRYSTAL HEALING FOR THE CHAKRAS

2.   Place your crystal on the floor either between your legs or under the chair. This is for the Earth Star Chakra.

3.   Visualise yourself as being a large strong tree with roots going deep into the Earth.

4.   See your roots reaching the very centre of the Earth where they wrap around a large Iron crystal.

5.   Next with both hands hold your crystal in the position of your Root Chakra. Close your eyes and hold it there for about a minute or longer if you wish.

6.   Continue raising the crystal up through all the Major Chakras. Spending about a minute with each one.

7.   For the Soul Star Chakra you will have to hold it with both hands about 6" above the head. Your arms will form a circular shape.

8.   Once finished put the crystal down safely. Raise your arms and shake them out.

9.   Open your eyes and take a few moments before getting up again.

How to Balance Your Chakras with a Crystal Point or Wand

Working on yourself with a Crystal Point or Crystal Wand is more involved than using a Chakra Crystal Set. You may of course get a like-minded friend to use the crystal on your chakras.

1.   Sit down with your legs crossed or on a chair while holding your crystal in your dominant hand.

2.   Close your eyes and take a few deep breaths.

3.   Visualise yourself as being a large strong tree with roots going deep into the Earth.

4.   See your roots reaching the very centre of the Earth where they wrap around a large Iron crystal.

5.   Open your eyes, lower your hand and point your crystal down towards the floor to the location of the Earth Star Chakra somewhere below your feet.

6.   In a small clockwise circular motion direct your crystal towards this chakra for about one minute or longer if you wish.

7.   Next move to the Root Chakra, You can point the crystal inwards now towards this area and again use circular motions for about a minute.

8.   Continue up through all the Major Chakras, balancing them one by one. For the Crown Chakra you can point the crystal downward towards the top of your head.

9.   For the Soul Star Chakra point the crystal upwards, just above the top of your head directing it in a circular motion as before. Take a few moments before getting up again.

How to Balance Your Chakras with a Single Crystal in Meditation

You can use any form of chakra balancing crystal. With a natural Crystal Point or Crystal Wand, have the crystal pointing upwards in your hands.

1.   Sit down with your legs crossed or on a chair and close your eyes.

2.   Hold your crystal in your hands on your lap and take a few deep breaths.

3.   Visualise yourself as being a large strong tree with roots going deep into the Earth.

4.   See your roots reaching the very centre of the Earth where they wrap around a large Iron crystal.

5.   Focus on the crystal you are holding and visualise it begin to glow with light.

6.   Visualise a luminous ball of soft white light descending onto your Soul Star Chakra. For about a minute see this ball of light surrounding this chakra.

7.   Now see the ball of light moving down onto the Crown Chakra. Repeat this process down through all the chakras. Spending about a minute with each one.

8.   Lastly visualise the ball of light descending down into the centre of the Earth.

9.   Open your eyes and take a few moments before getting up again.

9

CHAKRA HACKS: CRYSTALS THAT ALIGN ALL THE CHAKRAS

When your chakras are aligned they will be all lined up with each other. Your chakras system will be fully connected to the centre of the Earth, the greater Universe and your higher self. This allows for the greater flow of divine energy and wisdom to come through you.

Chakra alignment can help you feel more connected, present and better able to handle anything that comes your way. This is something you may wish to do after you have cleared and balanced your chakras.

The following selection of crystals and crystal healing methods will align and connect all your chakras.

Boji Stones

Usable Forms:

Unpolished crystals

Description:

Genuine Boji Stones come with a yellow certificate. They are small earthy rough and heavy disc shaped stones. They normally come as balanced pairs, one male and one female. Boji Stones also have an unusual magnetic polarity.

Aligning Properties:

Through their polarised energy signature Boji Stones draw your energy towards your core and anchor it like a magnetic iron bar.

Faden Quartz

Usable Forms:

Unpolished Crystal

Description:

These are flat double terminated clear Quartz crystals. Inside the crystals is a single ribbon like white band that runs horizontally through the centre of the crystal.

Aligning Properties:

Soothing Faden Quartz brings all the chakras back into alignment. It connects the Chakra System to the Earth's core and the centre of the Galaxy.

Black Tourmaline

Usable Forms:

Crystal Point, Tumble Stone

Description:

Tourmaline grows into long crystal points usually with three sides. If left unpolished it will have grooves or striations on the sides. Black Tourmaline is jet black and opaque.

Aligning Properties:

Black Tourmaline allows for the free flow of energy up and down the chakras. This stone firmly anchors your aura and energy body with the Earth's natural energy field.

Spectrolite

Usable Forms:

Tumble Stone, Polished Stone

Description:

Genuine Spectrolite is a unique variety of Labradorite only found in Finland. It is black with intense and metallic colours, which shift and shine when it catches the light. Unlike common grey Labradorite it can be found in all colours of the spectrum.

Aligning Properties:

Spectrolite anchors the light emanating from the chakras and realigns it with your spiritual core, Earth and the Galaxy. Spectrolite also balances the chakras.

Chrysanthemum Stone

Usable Forms:

Tumble Stone, Polished Stone

Description:

These black stones have a white flower like pattern. They look like flower fossils but the star burst pattern is actually formed by crystal formations within the stone.

Aligning Properties:

Chrysanthemum Stone is deeply grounding. It draws your energy down into the heart of the Earth. Aligning your chakras with the body and skeletal system.

Ways to Use Crystals to Align all the Chakras

Wearing or carrying these crystals will help keep your chakras aligned. The most effective method to use these crystals is to put them directly into the chakras or use them in meditation.

Please note that you can use a single crystal or a pair of the same crystals for chakra alignment. Boji Stones for example come in pairs but you could also use a pair of Chrysanthemum Stones if you wish. When working with pairs of crystals follow the instructions below but have one crystal in each hand.

Working with Chakra Crystal Sets

You can also use any of the chakra aligning crystals in this chapter for the position of the Earth Star Chakra in a Chakra Crystal Set. While doing Chakra balancing and clearing with a Chakra Crystal Set (as explained in Chapter 5) you will now also be aligning all your chakras at the same time.

The other way is to hold a pair of the chakra aligning crystals while you're doing chakra balancing and clearing with a Chakra Crystal Set. These methods are ideal when you do not know what is most needed or want to cleanse, balance and align all your chakras in one session.

How to Align Your Chakras with Crystals (Laying Down)

As with selecting crystals for a Chakra Crystal Set make sure your crystal has at least one flat side so that it can be laid on the body securely. If the crystal you have does not come as a

Tumble Stone use a polished or unpolished crystal.

1.   Find a quiet comfortable place to lie down.

2.   Place your crystal or crystals about 6" below your feet within the location of the Earth Star Chakra.

3.   Lay down facing up and get into a comfortable position. Take a few deep breaths.

4.   Close your eyes and visualise yourself as being a large strong tree with roots going deep into the Earth.

5.   See your roots reaching the very centre of the Earth where they wrap around a large Iron crystal.

6.   Sit up and move the crystal to your Root Chaka location. Lay back for a few seconds.

7.   Now slowly move the crystal up to the Sacral Chakra. Continue up the chakras pausing only for a few seconds.

8.   Lastly move the crystal about 6" above the top of your head for the Soul Star Chakra.

9.   Open your eyes and take a few moments before getting up again.

How to Align Your Chakras with Crystals (Sitting)

Similar to the method above but you will have to use your arms a little with this one.

1. Sit down with your legs crossed or on a chair and take a few deep breaths.

2. Place your crystal or crystals on the floor either between your legs or under the chair. This is for the Earth Star Chakra.

3. Visualise yourself as being a large strong tree with roots going deep into the Earth.

4. See your roots reaching the very centre of the Earth where they wrap around a large Iron crystal.

5. Next with both hands hold your crystal in the position of your Root Chakra. Pause for a few seconds.

6. Continue raising the crystal up through all the Major Chakras. Spending just a few seconds at each point.

7. For the Soul Star Chakra you will have to hold it with both hands about 6" above the head. Your arms will form a circular shape.

8. Once finished put the crystal down safely. Raise your arms and shake them out.

9.   Open your eyes and take a few moments before getting up again.

How to Align Your Chakras with Crystals in Meditation

1.   Sit down with your legs crossed or on a chair and close your eyes.

2.   Hold your crystal or pair of crystals in your hands on your lap and take a few deep breaths.

3.   Visualise yourself as being a large strong tree with roots going deep into the Earth.

4.   See your roots reaching the very centre of the Earth where they wrap around a large Iron crystal.

5.   Focus on the crystal you are holding and visualise it begin to glow with light.

6.   Visualise a beam of white light projecting downwards from your crystal towards the centre of the Earth.

7.   Now see a beam of light shining upwards from your crystal through all your chakras up into the sky.

8.   Lastly visualise this pillar of white light and feel your chakras aligning.

9.   When this feels complete, open your eyes and take a few moments before getting up again.

AFTERWARDS

I hope this book was given you a better understanding of the Chakra System and how it relates to all aspects of your life, mind, body and spirit. Understanding our chakras can become a big part of how you view the World and your spiritual practice. Crystal Healing is just one holistic key to unlocking the doorway to your energy body.

Over a period of time if you consistently cleanse, balance and align your chakras you will see changes in how you think, feel and manifest. Working with our chakras can be a transformational experience. Crystals can be powerful tools and allies on your own personal and spiritual growth.

If you enjoyed this book and found it helpful in any way, **please consider leaving me a short review on Amazon**. Your reviews are hugely helpful to me as an Independent Author and will help others be able to find this book in the search results.

With gratitude,

Ethan

ABOUT THE AUTHOR

Ethan Lazzerini is an author and blogger based in Yorkshire, England. He has been working with crystals for more than 25 years. Ethan works intuitively and practically with crystals to access the information and energy they hold. He believes crystals are spiritual tools and allies for personal development, spiritual growth, manifesting and psychic protection. In his books and popular blog articles, he aims to make Crystal Healing clear and easy to apply to everyday life.

When he is not writing, reading or hunting for crystals, he makes Crystal Healing jewellery for his successful jewellery line Merkaba Warrior. For lots of helpful Crystal Healing guides and tips, please visit his popular website and blog:

www.ethanlazzerini.com

Stay connected with Ethan Lazzerini on Social Media:

Facebook, Pinterest & Instagram

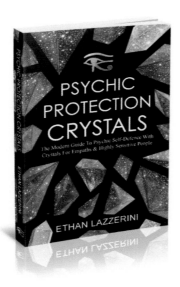

PSYCHIC PROTECTION CRYSTALS

The Modern Guide To Psychic Self-Defence With Crystals For Empaths & Highly Sensitive People

Do you take on the energy of others too easily? Are you constantly battling bad vibes? Have you ever experienced a psychic attack? In this book you will learn how to create strong and healthy energetic boundaries. Empower yourself with simple to advanced techniques to strengthen your aura and shield yourself from negative energies, toxic people and environments.

Meet the Guardians of the Mineral Kingdom. Explore over 50 crystals and their unique protective properties in detail. Supercharge your shielding, breeze past bad vibes and neutralise negative energies!

Available Now in Paperback & Kindle!

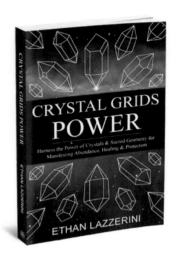

CRYSTAL GRIDS POWER

Harness the Power of Crystals & Sacred Geometry for Manifesting Abundance, Healing & Protection

Are you ready to tap into the healing energy and creative power of crystals? Discover how to harness the power of crystals and Sacred Geometry to amplify your intentions, focus your mind and manifest positive change in your life. Ethan Lazzerini uses over 25 years experience with crystals to formulate 34 intention based Crystal Grids for every purpose.

Explore the fascinating history and symbolism behind Crystal Grids. Clearly illustrated with diagrams and step-by-step instructions. This bestselling book contains EVERYTHING you need to know about Crystal Grids and how to make them. Includes FREE Printable Crystal Grid Templates to download!

Available Now in Paperback & Kindle!

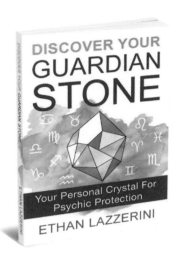

DISCOVER YOUR GUARDIAN STONE

Your Personal Crystal For Psychic Protection

If you subscribe to my monthly Crystal Newsletter and updates you will get this exclusive Ebook free. Learn how to use astrology to discover your personal go-to crystal for protection. Illustrated with full colour photos. This book is only available on my website by visiting the link below:

www.ethanlazzerini.com/freegift

Printed in Great Britain
by Amazon